GLORIA BAILEY-RAY

When To Get Up From The Table-When Love Is Not Being Served

AUTHENTICITY PRESS

First published by Authenticity Press 2025

Copyright © 2025 by Gloria Bailey-Ray

All rights reserved. No part of this publication may be reproduced, stored or transmitted in any form or by any means, electronic, mechanical, photocopying, recording, scanning, or otherwise without written permission from the publisher. It is illegal to copy this book, post it to a website, or distribute it by any other means without permission.

Gloria Bailey-Ray asserts the moral right to be identified as the author of this work.

Gloria Bailey-Ray has no responsibility for the persistence or accuracy of URLs for external or third-party Internet Websites referred to in this publication and does not guarantee that any content on such Websites is, or will remain, accurate or appropriate.

Designations used by companies to distinguish their products are often claimed as trademarks. All brand names and product names used in this book and on its cover are trade names, service marks, trademarks and registered trademarks of their respective owners. The publishers and the book are not associated with any product or vendor mentioned in this book. None of the companies referenced within the book have endorsed the book.

Second edition

ISBN: 978-1-7371583-4-9

*This book was professionally typeset on Reedsy.
Find out more at reedsy.com*

Dedication

To every woman who has ever lost her voice, dimmed her light, or stayed too long at a table where love was not being served—this is for you. May these words remind you of your worth, your power, and your right to rise. You are not broken; you are becoming. This book is your mirror, your permission, and your reminder that it's never too late to reclaim who you truly are. With fierce compassion, deep empathy, and unwavering belief in your next chapter, here's to you.

Gloria

"There comes a moment when staying becomes more painful than leaving. When silence feels like betrayal, and pretending costs more than the truth. To every soul who dared to rise after being diminished, dismissed, or devalued, you are the proof that healing is possible. You are the light you've been waiting for. Get up. Reclaim your place. Reclaim your power. The table was never meant to define you."

Gloria Bailey-Ray
Author

Contents

Foreword	iii
Preface	v
Acknowledgments	vii
Prologue	1
Introduction	3

I Part One

1	Wired For Connection	7
2	Rebound Relationships – A Dangerous Trap	11
3	Recognizing Repeated Patterns	16
4	Understanding Your Worth in a Relationship "When Your Shine...	21
5	Setting Expectations in a New Relationship	25
6	Abusive Relationships	31
7	Why People Cheat	37
8	Deciphering Friends with Benefits from a Booty Call	43
9	No Ring, No Rights	49
10	Recognizing Unhealthy Patterns Without Losing Yourself	55
11	Crossing Boundaries & Breaking Trust	60
12	A Loveless Relationship	64

13	When It's Not Progressing—It's Time to Pivot (and Peace Out)	70
14	The Moment of Liberation —When a Woman Gets Up From the...	75
15	When Love Isn't Being Served – Take Your Seat Somewhere Else	79
16	Author's Favorite Quotes	82

Epilogue	83
Afterword	85
About the Author	87

Foreword

Foreword

There comes a moment in all of our lives when we pause—not just out of fatigue or frustration, but from the quiet ache that whispers: *"This isn't who I am anymore."* That moment is sacred. It is often uncomfortable, sometimes heartbreaking, and always powerful. Because it is in that pause, that reckoning, that we start the journey back to ourselves.

When to Get Up From the Table: When Love Is Not Being Served is more than a book—it's a mirror. A soulful reflection of the courage it takes to walk away, not in anger, but in truth. To release what no longer fits and to reclaim what was never truly lost—your voice, your power, your peace.

Gloria Bailey-Ray does not write these words from a distance. She has lived them. Every chapter is infused with lived wisdom, hard-won clarity, and the grace that only comes from surviving what should have broken you, but didn't. This book doesn't offer shallow advice or quick fixes. Instead, it offers you a hand, a heartbeat, and a guide back to your own becoming.

Whether you are grieving the end of a relationship, recovering from betrayal, or simply ready to stop shrinking yourself to fit someone else's definition of love, this book is for you. It will challenge you to be honest, encourage you to be brave, and remind you that you are worthy of a life that feels like freedom.

In a world that too often tells women (and men) to endure, settle, and stay quiet, this book is your permission slip to get up. And not just get up but rise.

Turn these pages slowly. Revisit them as needed. Highlight the truths that speak to your soul. Because healing is not a one-time event—it's a return. A remembering. A revolution.

You are not alone. You are not too late. And you are not broken.

You are being reborn.

—Barbara A. Jackson

Preface

Preface

This book was born from both heartbreak and healing.

There was a season in my life when I gave everything I had to people and places that could not see me, love me, or honor me. I stayed at tables long after the nourishment was gone—hoping, praying, and pretending that things would change. I confused endurance with loyalty, silence with peace, and shrinking with strength. And like so many others, I learned that the hardest part isn't leaving—it's believing that you deserve to.

When to Get Up From the Table is not a manual on love or loss. It's a testimony of truth. A reflection of what happens when you finally get tired of waiting to be chosen and start choosing yourself. It's the deep exhale after holding your breath for too long.

I wrote this for the woman who whispers to herself at night, *"There has to be more than this."* For the man who shows up every day while silently unraveling. For the human heart that knows what it feels like to be dismissed, devalued, or denied—but still beats with hope. This book is for you.

Each chapter holds a part of my journey, but more importantly, it holds space for yours. You'll find stories, reflections, journal prompts, and affirmations designed not to fix you, but to remind you—you were never broken. You were simply conditioned to forget your power.

If you're reading this, you've already taken the first step toward your healing. And while the path may not be easy, I promise it is worth it. You are worth it.

Take your time with these pages. Let the truth settle where it needs to. Cry if you must. Scream if you need to. But most of all, let this be the moment you remember who you are.

You don't need permission to get up. You already have the power. This book is simply a mirror to show you what's been inside you all along.

With love, truth, and deep gratitude.

Authentically,
Gloria Bailey-Ray

Acknowledgments

Acknowledgments

Writing this book was not just a creative endeavor—it was a spiritual journey, an emotional reckoning, and a personal transformation. I could not have walked this path without a circle of strength, truth, and love around me.

To every woman who has ever sat at a table starving for love, recognition, or peace—you were in my heart as I wrote every word. You are the reason this book exists.

To the ones who saw me even when I couldn't fully see myself—thank you. Your belief in my voice gave me the courage to use it.

To my tribe—my siblings, "sista" girlfriends, friends, supporters, and mentors—your late-night talks, prayers, and unconditional love have been the scaffolding of my healing. You reminded me that it's okay to fall apart and still be worthy of everything whole.

To the women and men who have shared their stories with me over the years—you trusted me with your truth, and I carry that trust with care and reverence. This book reflects not only my journey but the universal ache and beauty of reclaiming oneself.

To my readers: whether this is your first step or your final chapter in healing, thank you for letting me walk beside you. I honor your bravery.

To the little girl inside of me who once believed she had to earn love by sacrificing herself—I see you now. I love you. And I promise never to abandon you again.

Finally, to the Divine Source that continually reminds me who I am and why I'm here—thank you for giving me the words when I had none, the strength when I was empty, and the fire when I felt forgotten.

This book is my offering. My release. My truth.

With all my heart,

Gloria Bailey-Ray

Prologue

Prologue

There comes a moment in every journey when silence is louder than words, and comfort becomes the mask of complacency. It's in that moment—when your spirit whispers that something isn't right—that the real work begins. *When To Get Up From The Table* isn't just a guide—it's a mirror. A mirror reflecting the spaces where you've overstayed, the relationships that have starved your joy, and the situations you've tolerated in the name of loyalty, love, or fear.

I know this intimately. As a single parent coming out of a painful divorce, I thought I had finally found the love of my life. Raised in a Christian home grounded in values and morals, going through a divorce was devastating in itself. So when love reappeared, I clung to it with hope—desperate for healing, believing that this time would be different.

But what followed was a storm I didn't see coming. I endured abuse, betrayal, lies, and manipulation. I missed the signs, ignored the warnings, and lost pieces of myself trying to make it work. Even after I left that relationship, I still didn't feel powerful enough to stand fully in my truth. It wasn't until I found myself with my leg broken in three places—physically shattered and emotionally depleted that I realized no one was coming to save me. I had to get up. I had to be my own advocate.

And when I did, everything changed. Clarity found me. Peace returned. And I finally understood the power of knowing *when to get up from the table.*

This book is not just my truth—it may be yours, too. It's for the woman who's stayed too long, the man who's settled for less, and the soul who's forgotten its worth. It's time to remember who you are and walk away from anything that doesn't honor that.

Pull up your chair—but only long enough to decide if what's being served is feeding your soul.

This is your invitation to examine your boundaries, your worth, and your voice. It's not about walking away in anger but rising with intention. Knowing when to get up from the table is about choosing yourself, unapologetically.

Let this be the beginning of your return to authenticity.

> **"You don't have to set yourself on fire to keep others warm."**
> — Unknown

Affirmation:

I am worthy of love, respect, and peace. I release anything that no longer serves my highest good. I give myself permission to walk away and stand tall in my truth.

Introduction

"Get Up From The Table" is a powerful metaphor for recognizing when a situation or relationship no longer serves your growth, peace, or worth. Just like walking away from a table where you're no longer being fed—emotionally, mentally, or spiritually—it signifies reclaiming your power and choosing self-respect over settling. It's a call to honor yourself enough to leave what no longer aligns with who you're becoming.

"The question isn't who's going to let me; it's who is going to stop me." —Ayn Rand

I

Part One

Gloria Bailey-Ray—Certified Professional Coach, speaker, and author—guides women and men to heal, rise, and walk in divine purpose. Known as "The Authentic Coach," she speaks truth with grace, helping others release what no longer serves them.

Her third book, When To Get Up From The Table, is a heartfelt invitation to reclaim your worth, listen to your soul, and choose yourself without apology. Gloria's message is simple but powerful: you are worthy, you are enough!

1

Wired For Connection

We are born in a relationship, we are wounded in a relationship, and we can be healed in a relationship." – Harville Hendrix.

The Human Need To be Seen and Held

We arrive in this world reaching not just for air, but for presence. Long before we speak our first words, we speak the language of connection. The warmth of a caregiver's arms, the responsiveness to our cries, the mirroring of our emotions— these early interactions become our silent instructors, forming our understanding of love, safety, and belonging.

This isn't just sentiment; it's science. Neuropsychology confirms that the human brain is a social organ molded by the people we bond with or fail to bond with. Our early relationships set the stage. They shape what psychologists call attachment patterns—internal blueprints that tell us whether intimacy feels safe or suffocating, whether vulnerability invites closeness or punishment.

The Hidden Lessons We Carry

Looking back on my own life—across personal, professional, and intimate relationships—I now see a thread I hadn't recognized at the time: a quiet but persistent need to be needed. A longing to be accepted. I confused being indispensable with being loved. I often asked, "What can I do to make them stay? instead of asking, Do I feel seen, valued, or safe here?

This need didn't come out of nowhere. It grew from invisible lessons learned in childhood—lessons about earning love, managing people's emotions, and being worthy only when useful. These are the unspoken survival strategies we pick up when love feels conditional. And as adults, we carry them like armor: over-giving, over-performing, shape-shifting.

Not because we're broken—but because at some point, those strategies kept us safe.

Still, underneath the performance, there's a deeper longing. We want someone to see us—beyond our roles, our output, or our polished exterior.

We want to be chosen, not out of duty, but with genuine delight.

We want a connection that feels like freedom, not sacrifice.

This longing is not a weakness. It's not clinginess. It's not a flaw. It is our most human need: to be known and loved for who we truly are.

Yet here lies the paradox: the very relationships we crave

can also stir our deepest fears. The closer someone gets, the more our protective instincts flare. We may pull away, over-accommodate,
numb out, or lash out—not because we don't care, but because we're afraid. Afraid of being hurt. Afraid of being abandoned. Afraid that we're not enough.

But awareness is the beginning of healing. When we learn to name these patterns without shame—when we notice our triggers and stay curious instead of critical—we begin to change the script. We stop operating from our wounds and start relating from our wholeness.
Love becomes less about proving ourselves and more about being ourselves.

Relationships will never be perfect. But they can be sacred spaces for growth, reflection, and repair. They are not about never messing up. They are about choosing to show up—even when it's messy, even when it's hard.

And here's the miracle: as we extend grace to our own messy, beautiful humanity, we grow more capable of loving others in theirs.
You don't have to be needed to be worthy.
You don't have to be perfect to be loved.
You only have to be real.

Journal Reflection

- Think back to your earliest memory of feeling either deeply connected or painfully disconnected from someone.
- What did that experience teach you — consciously or unconsciously — about what it means to be in a relationship?
- How might that early lesson still be showing up in your adult relationships today?

2

Rebound Relationships – A Dangerous Trap

There's a certain emptiness that settles in after a relationship ends—a silence that's hard to sit with. I used to run from that silence. I'd jump headfirst into the arms of someone new, telling myself I was moving on, when in truth, I was only *escaping.*

Looking back, I can see how often I tried to outrun the pain instead of sitting with it. I didn't want to feel the hurt, so I wrapped myself in the comfort of new attention, new energy, and the illusion of a fresh start. But each time I bypassed the healing, I found myself in, yet another relationship filled with familiar wounds. The same patterns. The same emotional weight. The same lessons—repeating, louder and harder.

That's the dangerous trap of a rebound relationship.

At its core, a rebound is less about love and more about distraction. It's the band-aid we slap over heartbreak, hoping it will keep the pain from seeping through. We tell ourselves we're fine. We smile. We keep moving. But inside, we haven't processed the grief, the loss, or the lessons. And unhealed pain has a way of disguising itself as chemistry, urgency, or even love.

Why We Rush Into the Rebound

People enter rebound relationships for many reasons. I've lived through most of them:

- **Avoiding heartbreak.** I didn't want to feel the ache of loneliness.
- **Seeking validation.** I wanted to prove I was still desirable, lovable, chosen.
- **Filling a void.** I was uncomfortable with solitude, so I filled the space with someone—*anyone.*
- **Getting revenge.** I wanted to be seen, missed, envied. I thought if I moved on first, I would win.

But there is no winning when the heart is still wounded. There's only postponing the healing.

What Really Happens in a Rebound

Rebound relationships may feel exciting at first, even intoxicating. But beneath the rush lies instability. When I didn't take the time to process my previous relationship, I carried its baggage into the next one—unaware, unhealed, and emotionally unavailable.

Here's what I learned the hard way:

1. **You can't skip grief.** You can delay it, distract from it, deny

it—but eventually, it will demand your attention.
2. **Unprocessed pain becomes the architect of your future.** If you don't examine it, you'll unknowingly recreate it.
3. **The new partner isn't a cure.** They deserve your presence, not your projections.

I expected new people to make me forget the old pain. But no one else could do the work I was avoiding. And when they couldn't "fix" me or fill the void, I resented them—or I withdrew. It wasn't fair to them, and it wasn't kind to me.

Signs You Might Be in a Rebound Relationship

Not every new relationship after a breakup is a rebound. But if you're moving fast and feeling emotionally numb or confused, take a moment to reflect. You may be in a rebound if:

- You're still emotionally entangled with your ex (longing, anger, sadness).
- You're using your new partner as a comparison or distraction.
- You've rushed into commitment too quickly.
- You feel emotionally disconnected but physically attached.
- The relationship is about *relief*, not *real connection*.

How to Break the Pattern

I had to learn that healing isn't about time—it's about intention. I had to stop using people to bandage my wounds and start asking myself the deeper questions:

- *What am I afraid to feel?*
- *What part of me still needs care, forgiveness, or closure?*
- *What did my past relationship teach me about myself?*

Here's what helped me reclaim my wholeness:

1. **Give yourself permission to pause.** Healing requires space. Don't rush it.
2. **Reconnect with who you are outside of a relationship.** Discover your joy again.
3. **Be honest—with yourself and others.** If you're not ready for love, say so.
4. **Don't fear solitude.** Learn to be at peace in your own company.
5. **Seek closure.** Not just with your ex, but with the part of yourself that accepted less than you deserved.

When Are You Ready to Love Again?

You'll know you're ready not when you crave love, but when you *can give it.*

- When your past no longer defines you.
- When being alone feels empowering, not empty.
- When you see a new person as a whole human—not a healer, savior, or distraction.
- When you're ready to grow together, not hide together.

Rebound relationships taught me that healing is not optional—it's necessary. Until I turned inward and faced the ache, I couldn't build anything real with someone else.

- You don't have to rush your healing to prove you're okay.
- You don't have to run to someone else to avoid yourself.
- The most courageous thing you can do is pause, breathe, and choose yourself first.

- That's not loneliness. That's liberation.

Final Thoughts

Rebound relationships may seem like a quick fix for heartbreak, but they often cause more harm than good. Instead of rushing into something new, take the time to heal, grow, and reconnect with yourself. A meaningful and lasting relationship will come when you're emotionally ready, not when you're trying to fill a void.

If you're coming out of a breakup, give yourself grace. Healing takes time, and self-love is the best foundation for any future relationship.

Journal Reflection:

Think about a time when you entered a new relationship soon after a breakup.

- What motivated you to move on quickly?
- Were you seeking connection, distraction, validation, or healing?
- In hindsight, what did you learn about yourself from that experience?
- What does "emotional readiness" look like for you today?
- Are there emotional patterns you tend to repeat in relationships, such as over-giving, avoiding conflict, choosing emotionally unavailable partners, or fearing abandonment?
- "What would it look like to respond differently next time?" ("Understanding Yourself: Explore the Why Behind Your Actions")

3

Recognizing Repeated Patterns

I jumped out of the frying pan and landed straight into the fire.

After divorcing my first husband, I thought I was running toward a fresh start. A new beginning. I packed up my life, relocated cities, and almost walked down the aisle with someone I barely knew—hoping, praying, convincing myself that this time, it would be different.

But what I didn't realize then was this: when you don't take the time to heal, to truly examine the wounds and the why—you don't move forward. You *repeat.* You recreate the same patterns in new packaging.

I didn't know he was unhealed. I didn't know abuse was something he had witnessed and internalized. I didn't know I was stepping into a cycle I had already lived through, this time with a different face and a new zip code. I had mistaken movement for progress. But emotionally, I was still right where I'd left off—confused, hopeful, desperate to feel loved. And in that desperation, I abandoned the most important relationship of all: the one I had with myself.

The Moment of Reckoning

There comes a moment in every woman's life when she must face a hard truth:

Am I choosing myself, or am I abandoning myself to keep someone else comfortable?

I had stayed before. I stayed for the image. I stayed for the illusion of stability. I stayed for the hope that he'd change. But change never came. And now, I had done it again—only this time, I couldn't pretend I didn't see it coming.

Let's not sugarcoat it:

- When your partner cheats and lies repeatedly...
- When children are born outside your union...
- When words become weapons and silence becomes punishment...
- When he touches you only when he wants something, and disappears when life gets hard...

That is not love. That is not commitment. That is not a sacred partnership. That is survival dressed up as marriage. And I was tired of surviving.

Recognizing the Signs

I wish I could say I saw it right away. But the truth is, I made excuses—because that's what I had been taught. Women are conditioned to fix, to stay, to hold things together even when they're falling apart. But here's what I now know to be true:

Repeated patterns are red flags. Not isolated incidents. Not

bad days. ***Patterns.***
Here's what I had to call out by name:

- Infidelity wasn't a mistake. It was a habit.
- Verbal abuse wasn't stress. It was control.
- Emotional neglect wasn't forgetfulness. It was disregard.
- No accountability meant no intention to change.
- Lack of partnership left me doing it all—while he disappeared.
- Booty call energy kept me emotionally starved but physically expected.
- Disrespect masked as dominance, jokes, and silence.
- Unhealed trauma he refused to face, while mine kept bleeding out.

It was all right there—on replay. And I finally saw it.

Why We Stay

I didn't stay because I was weak. I stayed because I had been taught that something is better than nothing. That a half-love was better than no love. That being chosen, even by someone unworthy, was better than being alone.

But I was wrong.

You are not too much. You are just asking the wrong person.

The thing I feared the most—being alone—was actually the very thing that saved me.

The Deciding Factor

So, when do you leave? When do you finally get up from the table?

- You leave the moment staying feels like self-betrayal.
- You get up when your soul is shrinking in his presence.
- You get up when your voice is muted and your boundaries are erased.
- You get up when the cost of pretending becomes heavier than the fear of being on your own.
- You get up when your children start to believe that this is what love looks like—and you know it isn't.
- And most of all, you get up when you remember who the hell you are.
- Not a fixer. Not a sacrifice.
- But a whole woman. A truth-teller. A warrior.
- I didn't know everything back then. But I know now:
- Healing isn't optional. Self-respect is non-negotiable.
- And love that costs you is far too expensive.

Journal Reflection

- Have I been making excuses for repeated behaviors that go against my values or well-being?
- What have I normalized in this relationship that would horrify the woman I once was — or the woman I want to become?
- What am I afraid will happen if I leave? And what am I afraid will happen if I stay?
- What does "choosing myself" actually look like at this moment?
- What support systems do I need to get up from the table and not look back?

"The moment you decide that you are no longer available for pain disguised as love... is the moment you begin to rise."

4

Understanding Your Worth in a Relationship "When Your Shine Becomes a Threat"

I didn't always know what I was worth. I knew how to work. I knew how to lead. I knew how to survive. But understanding my value in a relationship? That took years—and a lot of heartache—to figure out.

Men and women have always been drawn to my shine. They were attracted to my confidence, my hustle, my ability to walk into a room and own it. But never stayed long enough to grow beside me. I was raised in a small, tight-knit Christian town where you were taught to be kind, polite, and humble. But nobody warned me about what happens when you step into a city full of fast talkers and slow walkers—men who say all the right things but carry all the wrong intentions.

I wasn't prepared for that. Not emotionally. Not spiritually. And definitely not relationally.

I left home with hope and high standards, but in the city—let's call it what it was, a sea of piranhas—I had to learn the hard way that not everyone who claps for you is in your corner. I didn't recognize the signs. I thought love meant proving I was worthy. I gave too much too soon. Too many came for the glow, but not the growth.

And time after time, I found myself in relationships where once they had me, they tried to **dim me**.

Are You Being Loved or Just Tolerated?

There comes a point when you have to pause and ask yourself: Am I being genuinely loved, or just temporarily entertained? Am I valued for who I am, or simply used for what I provide?

One of the biggest mistakes I made was giving ***wife energy*** to men who only brought ***boyfriend crumbs***. I gave support, loyalty, encouragement—and in return, I got silence, excuses, and manipulation disguised as love.

But here's the truth I had to finally claim: ***My worth is not up for negotiation.***

Let's be clear:

You do not need to raise a man. You need to be with one.

Love Yourself Enough to Leave!

I've been the chef, the Uber driver, the therapist, and the life coach—in relationships that left me running on empty. I gave so much trying to prove I was "ride or die" when all he ever did was ride... while I died inside.

But I woke up. I remembered who I was. And I decided: **No more discounts on my destiny.**

You are not here to carry a man's potential while neglecting your peace.

You are not here to be someone's fallback plan while they "figure it out."

You are not here to shrink so he can shine.

So, stop:

- Giving wife benefits to someone who won't even claim you properly.
- Shrinking yourself to fit into his broken vision of manhood.
- Waiting for him to "grow up" while your soul grows weary.

You are the prize. You are the peace. You are the woman who sets the standard.

And when it's clear that he doesn't value you, don't just sit there. **Get up!**

Journal Reflection

- Am I giving more than I receive in my current or past relationships?
- In what ways have I lowered my standards or silenced my needs to keep someone around?
- What does a relationship rooted in mutual effort and respect look like to me?
- If I'm being honest with myself, is the person I'm with showing up as a partner or as a passenger?
- What would loving myself enough to walk away look like in action?

WHEN TO GET UP FROM THE TABLE-WHEN LOVE IS NOT BEING SERVED

5

Setting Expectations in a New Relationship

From Silence to Self-Honor

After everything I had been through—the disappointments, the betrayals, the repeated cycles—I reached a breaking point. Or maybe, more truthfully, it was a *becoming* point.

I stopped running. I stopped trying to fix anyone else.

I stopped shrinking to fit inside someone else's comfort zone. And instead, I sat still.

For once, I just sat *with myself.* No noise. No distractions. No fake smile.

Just me, my truth, and the silence that scared me more than any heartbreak ever had.

But in that silence, something powerful happened. I started to *hear myself again.*

And I began to write—not out of loneliness, but out of clarity.

I wrote down exactly what I wanted in a partner.

What I *needed* in a husband. What kind of man would I trust to help raise my two children, not just be present but be present *with purpose?*

I wrote about the love I deserved. The protection I needed. The softness I longed for, and the strength I could lean on.

No more guesswork. No more hoping he'd read my mind.

No more settling for someone who was impressed by my glow but threatened by my fire.

This chapter of my life wasn't about finding a man.

It was about finding *my standards*—and refusing to lower them again.

Speak What You Seek

A new relationship is exciting. Hopeful. Emotional.

But without clarity, excitement becomes confusion, and hope turns into heartbreak.

The biggest lesson I learned?

Expectations aren't burdens. They're boundaries with a voice.

They are the way we tell someone:

- "This is how I deserve to be loved."
- "This is what I bring to the table."
- "This is how I expect to be treated—and how I will treat you."

If they can't hear that now, they're not ready for *you.*

Communicate with Courage

You can't be afraid to name what you need.

You can't hope someone guesses what makes you feel safe or

loved.

Talk about your values.

Talk about your triggers.

Talk about how you fight, how you forgive, how you feel seen.

Real love grows in truth.

If they care for you, they'll want to learn your heart, not just your body.

Set Boundaries, Not Walls. Boundaries are not threats. They are invitations—to love you *right.* They protect your peace. Your time. Your emotional safety.

When I wrote my list, I included:

- No tolerance for emotional neglect or infidelity.
- Respect for my autonomy and my role as a mother.
- A desire for spiritual growth together, not domination.
- Shared responsibility and shared vision.

That list became my compass.

It reminded me of who I was, so I wouldn't lose myself in who someone else *could be.*

Talk about the future early

Some people will say it's "too soon" to talk about marriage, family, or life vision.

But here's what I know: if I'm investing my time, my heart, and bringing you around my children—*we're going to talk about where this is going.*

You don't owe anyone silence about your future.

Talk about your dreams.

Talk about partnership.

Talk about how you both define love, and if those definitions match.

Clarity now saves heartbreak later.

Compromise Without Contorting

Yes, compromise matters. But compromising your soul? Your safety? Your voice? Not!

I will adjust my schedule.

I will consider your needs.

But I will not bend until I'm unrecognizable just to make someone stay.

If compromise feels like betrayal, it's not love. It's a sacrifice. And love shouldn't cost you... *you.*

Know When to Walk Away

You can communicate clearly. You can set boundaries. You can express your dreams and still find yourself with someone who refuses to meet you there. That's when you choose peace over potential.

Walk away if:

- They ignore your needs and dismiss your voice.
- They view boundaries as insults, not guidelines.
- They won't grow, won't try, and won't listen.
- Their version of love requires you to shrink.

Walking away isn't failure....**It's *freedom.***

Final Reflection: Write the List. Then Live It.

I wrote that list in stillness.

And it became a sacred promise to myself:

Never again would I love someone more than I respected myself.

Never again would I pour from an empty cup just to be chosen.

So, if you're in a new relationship—or healing from an old one—sit down.

Get quiet. Ask your spirit what it truly desires. And write it down.

You deserve a love that honors your growth, not your wounds.

A love that feels like a partnership, not parenthood.

A love that protects your children as fiercely as it protects your peace.

You don't just need love. **You need the *right* love.**

And when the right one shows up, they'll recognize that list, not as a demand, but as a *divine invitation.*

And they'll say: **"I see you. I honor you. Let's build together."**

Journal Reflection

- What are the most important expectations that I have for myself and my partner in a relationship?
- Where have I historically compromised too much, and how did it affect me?
- What boundaries will I set and communicate clearly in my next or current relationship?
- What expectations feel non-negotiable to me?

- Am I currently honoring my expectations or settling?

6

Abusive Relationships

When Pain Wears a Familiar Face

I never imagined I'd be the woman with a black eye—especially not six months pregnant.

I was carrying life inside of me, and the man who was supposed to love and protect me had turned violent. One swing. One moment. One trauma I'd never forget.

You'd think that would be the end of it. But abuse is rarely just one moment.

It's a pattern. A cycle. And sometimes, it returns to your doorstep even after you leave.

Years later, though we were no longer together, I still had to share custody with him. He still had access. Still had proximity. Still had *permission*, in the eyes of the law, to stay tethered to my life. And then it happened again: he broke my leg in three places. Three.

And do you know what the system did? Nothing. He wasn't

arrested. It was brushed off. Treated like a spat. As if the bruises were just misunderstandings and the broken bones were a lovers' quarrel. But I wasn't just humiliated. I was devastated. Because my kids saw it all. And when your oldest child looks you in the eye and says, **"I wanted to kill him for what he did to you,"** a part of your soul crumbles. No child should have to carry that kind of rage. No child should have to carry *my* pain.

Why Leaving Wasn't Just About Me

I didn't just leave for myself. I left for them.

I saw what it did to my children—the confusion, the fear, the silence in their eyes when words failed. Abuse doesn't just harm bodies. It imprints trauma into the atmosphere of the home. It poisons the innocence of children. And it distorts their understanding of what love is *supposed* to be.

I stayed longer than I should have. Out of fear. Out of hope. Out of the lie that maybe he'd finally change. But change never came. Only more bruises. More betrayal. More broken pieces to pick up in silence.

What Abuse Looks Like—Beyond the Bruises

Abuse isn't always fists. Sometimes, it's words that cut deeper than any punch.

Sometimes, it's isolation. Manipulation. Gaslighting. Control.

It's him showing up at the house unannounced and no one holding him accountable. It's sharing custody with your abuser and pretending to co-parent when all you want is safety. It's

The Cost of Staying

Abuse cost me more than broken bones. It cost me confidence. It cost me peace.

It nearly cost me my children's emotional well-being. Even when we think we're shielding them, they *know*. They hear the slammed doors. They see the tears we cry behind bathroom sinks. They feel the tension, the fear, the exhaustion. And one day, they'll tell you. My son did. And it broke me.

The Reality of Leaving

Leaving wasn't easy.

I didn't have a plan at first—just the knowing that I *had* to go.

I had to choose safety over shame.

Healing over history.

Freedom over fear.

And yes, it was hard. I had to rebuild.

Physically. Emotionally. Financially.

But nothing—and I mean *nothing*—is harder than staying in a space that breaks you.

To the Woman Who's Still There

I see you. I know how terrifying it is to imagine life without him.

I know how exhausting it is to keep hiding the bruises, physical or emotional.

I know how the world tries to guilt you into staying "for the kids" while ignoring what staying *does* to the kids.

You are not crazy. You are not weak. And you are not alone.

There are shelters. There are hotlines. There are people who will believe you.

You don't need more time. You need a plan. And you *deserve* to live.

Final Thought: You Are Not What He Did

What he did to you does not define you. The bruises will fade. The bones will heal. The shame will lift. But only if you *go.*

Not just physically—but mentally, emotionally, spiritually.

You have to unlearn every lie he fed you about your worth.

You have to believe you're worthy of peace, protection, and unconditional love.

Let me say this again for the woman who needs to hear it:

You are not broken. You are not too much.

You are not responsible for his rage.

You are a survivor.

And you are *allowed* to get up from the table—especially when the meal has always come with pain.

Journal Reflection: Reclaiming My Voice

Take a quiet moment for yourself. Breathe deeply and allow your heart and mind to speak honestly. This space is just for you.

- When I think about "safety," what feelings come up for me?
- What does safety look and feel like in my life right now?
- How has being in or witnessing an abusive relationship affected how I see myself?
- What beliefs about myself have I carried that might not belong to me?
- What are three things I would say to a close friend who was in my situation?
- Can I say those same things to myself—with compassion?
- What does respect mean to me in a relationship?
- Write down five qualities or boundaries that represent respect for you.
- I deserve…
- Complete this sentence multiple times. Don't hold back. Write what you truly deserve—emotionally, physically, spiritually.
- Who or what in my life reminds me that I am not alone?
- List your sources of strength, even if they are books, songs, memories, or faith.
- One small step I can take this week toward reclaiming my power is…
- No matter how small—every step matters.

Let this reflection be a safe space for your truth to unfold. Healing isn't linear, but every time you write, reflect, and show up for yourself, you take back your power, piece by piece.

WHEN TO GET UP FROM THE TABLE-WHEN LOVE IS NOT BEING SERVED

7

Why People Cheat

The Pain Behind the Smile

People always ask, "How did you not see the signs?"

The truth is, sometimes you're too tired to see anything but what's right in front of you.

When you're a single mother working two jobs, trying to keep the lights on, meals cooked, homework done, and your own tears at bay—you don't have the luxury of decoding lies or dissecting red flags. You are in survival mode, and survival doesn't leave much room for intuition.

That's where I was. Exhausted. Overextended. Doing it *all*—while getting absolutely no financial help from the fathers of my children.

I wasn't ignoring the signs. I just didn't have the capacity to hold one more disappointment. So, I kept going. I told myself everything was fine. I believed what I needed to believe just to make it through the week.

But eventually, the truth breaks through. And when it does, it shatters everything.

Why People Cheat – From the Outside In

Cheating isn't always about lust.

It's about *lack*—and that lack can live inside the cheater long before they ever meet you.

Here are some of the most common reasons people cheat:

1. Emotional Emptiness

Some cheat because they feel unseen or emotionally neglected. They want to feel desired, important, and special. But instead of doing the work within their relationship—or themselves—they reach outside.

2. Physical Disconnect

For others, it's about physical dissatisfaction or mismatched desires. Instead of having a tough conversation, they chase pleasure somewhere else.

3. Temptation and Weakness

Sometimes, it's not about a plan—it's about a moment. A trip. A message. A door they choose to walk through without thinking of what's on the other side.

4. Revenge

They're hurt, so they hurt back. But revenge cheating doesn't heal wounds. It just multiplies the damage.

5. Boredom or Fear of Monotony

Some people are addicted to the thrill of "new." Commitment feels like a cage. And instead of being honest, they cheat to feel free—while keeping you on lockdown.

6. Insecurity and Validation-Seeking
They cheat because they don't feel good enough. Ironically, they make others feel not enough just to fill their own emptiness.

7. Addictive Behavior
Cheating becomes a pattern. A compulsion. A form of escape that grows into an addiction—emotional, physical, or both.

8. Learned Behavior
Many cheaters were exposed to infidelity growing up. They normalize betrayal because it's all they've ever known.

The Cost of Missing the Signs
When I finally looked back with clear eyes, I saw the signs.
The detachment. The lies that didn't quite line up. The coldness masked as "tired."
The shift in routine. The "late nights" and "business trips."

But at the time, I was too busy figuring out how to stretch a dollar, cook dinner, and fold laundry at 2 AM. I was too busy surviving. And survival sometimes mutes your instincts.

Because of the truth? It's not just cheating that breaks your heart—it's how long you have to *pretend* you didn't feel it.

The Ripple Effect of Betrayal
Cheating doesn't just hurt the betrayed partner. It ripples out like a stone dropped in still water.

- It wounds your children. They may not understand what's happening, but they feel the fallout.
- It damages your self-worth. You start asking what you did wrong.
- It breeds shame. Not just because they cheated, but because you stayed.
- It isolates. You stop talking to people because you don't want them to know.
- It repeats. If not confronted and healed, the pattern shows up again and again.

When the Pain Becomes Your Teacher

Infidelity cracked something in me. But it also uncovered something:

My boundaries.

My worth.

My right to be loved with honesty and care.

I used to think loyalty meant holding on no matter what.

Now I know real loyalty starts with *me*.

Journal Reflection: Navigating the Wounds of Infidelity

Take a quiet moment with yourself. This reflection is not about judgment—it's about truth, clarity, and healing.

Personal Experience or Observation

- Have you ever experienced or witnessed infidelity in a relationship?
- If so, what emotions arose in you—anger, grief, confusion, betrayal, or something else?

- Write about what you saw and felt and how it changed your perception of relationships.

Trust and Vulnerability

- What does trust mean to you in a relationship?
- Have you ever found it difficult to trust again after being hurt? Why or why not?

Exploring the "Why"

- Think about the reasons people cheat.
- Can you see how emotional dissatisfaction, fear of commitment, or low self-esteem might lead someone to stray—even if it doesn't justify it?
- Have you ever sought validation outside a relationship (romantic or otherwise)? What were you truly needing at the time?

Long-Term Impact

- What are the long-term effects of betrayal that you've noticed in yourself or others?
- Do you feel any lingering wounds—fear of being left, fear of being lied to, or doubting your worth?

Your Healing Path

- What does healing look like for you if you've been betrayed?
- If you've ever hurt someone, how did you seek redemption or understanding?

- What boundaries or values do you now hold sacred in your relationships?

Affirmation:

"I honor my feelings and experiences, and I give myself permission to heal, grow, and love with wisdom."

8

Deciphering Friends with Benefits from a Booty Call

Is There a Difference?

Let's be real: at a certain point in life, especially when you're working two jobs, managing a household, raising children alone, and barely finding time to breathe, the last thing you need is confusion disguised as companionship.

After the heartbreak, the betrayal, the empty promises, I found myself standing at the intersection of "What is this?" and "What am I doing here?"

The so-called "Friends with Benefits" phase? That blurred line where they want your body, maybe your laugh, but not your life.

The late-night "u up?" texts? That wasn't flirtation. It was convenience.

Booty calls? They didn't care what I did that day or how tired I was. They cared about one thing—and one thing only.

Thank goodness I had the wisdom (and the fear) to pause and

ask myself:

Is this the love I've been praying for? Or am I just too exhausted to demand more?

And let's not forget this wasn't just about loneliness or longing—it was about life and death.

Because I wasn't just afraid of getting my heart broken again.

I was afraid of contracting something that could end my life.

Permanency and *stability* were not luxuries for me—they were *necessities.*

Friends with Benefits vs. Booty Call: What's the Difference? Here's the truth: not much.

Both may come with shared laughs and late-night thrills, but neither promises roots, respect, or reliability.

The difference? One might ask how your day went. The other just wants to know if you're free.

And when you're a single mom trying to hold your world together, **you don't need someone who wants your body without carrying your burdens.**

The Signs Were Always There

But back then, I didn't always see them—not because I was blind, but because I was busy.

Busy folding laundry at midnight.

Busy figuring out how to stretch one paycheck across two weeks.

Busy showing up for everyone... while no one was showing up for me.

So, when someone showed interest, even if it was lazy interest, I wanted to believe it was real. But deep down, I knew real love doesn't live in the shadows of convenience.

6 Signs You're Not in a Relationship—You're in Rotation

- The "Text-Only" Syndrome-They don't call. They don't check in. They just show up with emojis, "wyd?" and 2 a.m. alerts.
- A partner plans. A placeholder pings.
- No Real Dates, No Real Depth-If all you do is meet in private, behind closed doors, on their terms, you're not dating. You're donating your time to someone who has no intention of investing.
- The Vanishing Act-They disappear. Reappear. Act like nothing happened.
- When you ask real questions, they give vague answers. If they're hiding from your truth, they're not ready for your love.
- Emotional Unavailability-They avoid deep talks. They laugh at your feelings. They keep you compartmentalized.

A person who wants to build with you invites you into their world, not just their bed.

Ask Yourself: What Do You Really Want?

Do you want to feel desired... or respected?

Do you want attention... or intention?

Do you want someone for the night... or someone for the journey?

Do you want to feel like a Priority, not an Option?

Friends with benefits might offer momentary excitement, but they rarely lead to mutual fulfillment.

Booty calls? Even less.

I wasn't interested in moments anymore. I wanted **legacy**.

I wanted someone who would not just undress my body but understand my soul.

Someone who didn't see my kids as baggage—but as a blessing.

When Your Standards Save Your Life

They say love is a risk. But some risks come with too high a price. Risk without rewards, is it worth it?

Beyond the emotional damage, there's the physical risk. No casual fling is worth a lifetime of medical management or anxiety. If someone won't talk openly about protection, testing, and health, they're not protecting you.

When I thought about STIs—especially HIV, a lifelong condition that doesn't always show symptoms—I knew no fleeting passion was worth the possibility of devastating consequences.

So, I started doing what every woman should do:

Ask the hard questions. Set the firm boundaries. Say no when your spirit says no—even when your body is tempted to say yes.

Journal Reflection: Deciphering A Booty Call From a Relationship

Communication Patterns

- When do they usually reach out?
- How do you feel when you receive a late-night text?
- Do you have meaningful conversations outside of sex?

Time Spent Together

- What do your meetups actually involve?
- Do you share experiences beyond physical intimacy?

Consistency & Presence

- Do they vanish and return without explanation?
- Do they shy away from serious topics?
- Do you feel emotionally safe?

Emotional Depth

- Are your emotional needs acknowledged?
- Have you been integrated into their life in any real way?
- Are you hiding parts of yourself just to keep the connection alive?

Gut Check

- Do you feel like a priority—or a placeholder?

- How often do you bend to fit them, while they stay rigid?

Health & Safety

- Have you had honest conversations about protection and testing?
- Do you feel empowered or pressured?

Self-Assessment

- Are you hoping for more?
- Are you being honest about your needs?
- If nothing changed, would you be happy staying?

Choosing Yourself

- What does "being a memory, not a moment" mean to you?
- What boundaries will you set moving forward?

Affirmation:
"I am not a backup plan. I am not a convenience. I am a whole woman, worthy of love, loyalty, and lasting peace."

9

No Ring, No Rights

Decoding Boyfriend Status with Husband Privileges

Let me be real with you—I had to learn this the hard way. There was a season in my life when I thought love meant giving everything. My time. My energy. My car. My keys. My body. My heart. I didn't know I was auditioning for a role he never intended to give me. What I thought was love? It wasn't. And while I was trying to build a home, he was just looking for a place to crash.

Coming from a small town, raised in a God-fearing household, I wasn't taught to look for the red flags. I was taught to be kind, nurturing, and to make a man feel needed. But baby, let me tell you—there's a difference between being needed and being used. And I had to learn the difference while raising children, holding down two jobs, and still trying to keep a roof over our heads. I wasn't just tired. I was exhausted. And that's when they come in—men who sniff out your shine and want to dim it, not share in it.

The Liberty Takers: When "Help" Becomes Habit

Some men don't ask. They take. They take your peace. They take your car. They take up space in your house, your kitchen, and your spirit. And if you're not paying attention, they'll take your children's sense of safety too.

I've had men take liberties they never earned—eating meals I stretched to feed my kids, lounging in homes I was barely affording, asking for rides in cars they never helped maintain. I've had to stand between a man and my child, not just physically but emotionally. And when you've seen fear in your child's eyes because of someone you allowed in the door? That kind of shame doesn't fade easily. But it does sharpen you.

Wake-Up Calls Dressed as Struggle

- The Man Without a Plan: Living on someone's couch, always with a story, but never with a solution. Sis, being broke is a condition. Being comfortable with it is a character flaw. If he doesn't have a plan, don't let him rent space in yours.
- The Car Borrower: "Let me borrow your car real quick." He's running errands with your gas and pulling up on other women while you're working a double shift. If a man doesn't have his own ride and can't contribute to yours, why is he in your driver's seat—literally or figuratively?
- The Table Thief: Always ready to eat but never brings a bag of groceries. If he doesn't even bring paper towels to the home he's eating in, he's not a partner—he's a grown dependent.

- The Bare Minimum Bro: Never plans a date. Never contributes to bills. Never asks how your day was. Just vibes. And we're supposed to be grateful that he shows up? No, thank you, Ma'am!

When I Found My Voice

I remember the day I decided it had to stop. My kids deserved better. I deserved better. I stood in the mirror, looked myself in the eye, and said: You are not a man's last resort. You are the blessing he should be grateful for.

And let me tell you—when I started loving myself out loud, everything changed. I stopped accepting "potential" and started requiring presence. I stopped negotiating with red flags and started walking away at the first sign of disrespect. I stopped handing out husband privileges to men who hadn't even earned the title of "intentional."

Lessons Learned

- If he's not building, he's blocking.
- If he's always in need and never in service, he's not your partner.
- If he doesn't honor your children, your peace, or your dreams, he has no place in your life.
- And if he expects everything but offers nothing? Walk him to the door—then change the locks.

Final Thought: Love Doesn't Live in Handouts

Stop setting full-course meals for men who only bring appetite and excuses. You are not a stepping stone. You are the table, the meal, the blessing, the favor. If he can't match your energy, efforts, or standards, he doesn't get to sit with you.

Protect your peace. Defend your children's peace. And when a man shows you who he is—don't cook for him, don't care for him, don't carry him.

Get up. And let him eat somewhere else.

Journaling Reflection:
"The Moment You Get Up From the Table"
Reality Check: The State of the Relationship

- In what ways have you been giving more than you've been receiving in your current (or past) relationship?
- Have you been offering "wife-level" effort to someone who only shows up with "boyfriend-level" energy—or less?
- List the behaviors that made you question whether you were truly being loved, valued, and respected.

The Warning Signs: What Are You Tolerating?
Reflect on the types of men described in this chapter:

- Have you dated a "Man Without a Home"? What was his plan (if any)? Did you feel like you were building together or carrying him?
- Have you encountered "The Car Borrower" or "The Free Loader"? What did you feel in those moments—used, frustrated, taken for granted?
- Have you found yourself with a "Bare Minimum Boyfriend"? How did his lack of effort affect your sense of worth?

Write about moments when you ignored your intuition or made excuses for someone's lack of initiative.

Self-Awareness: Why Did You Stay?

- What part of you believed this was the best you could get at the time?
- Did you stay because of loneliness, potential, hope, fear of starting over—or all of the above?
- How did staying in that dynamic affect your self-esteem?

The Hard Questions: What Do You Deserve?

- Define what love, value, and respect look like to you in a relationship.
- What does reciprocity mean to you in real-life actions, not just words?
- What are your non-negotiables moving forward?

The Liberation: Getting Up From the Table

- What would it look like for you to stand up and walk away from a one-sided relationship?
- What emotions come up when you imagine choosing yourself?
- If you've already walked away, what have you gained since reclaiming your time, energy, and peace?

Affirm Yourself: I Am Worthy

Write your own affirmations based on this chapter. Here are a few to get you started:

- "I deserve a relationship where love is mutual, and effort is balanced."

- "I will no longer accept crumbs while offering a feast."
- "My worth is not determined by how much I can give to someone who gives me so little."

Your Next Step: What Will You Do With This Clarity?

Now that you've reflected honestly:

- What boundaries do you need to set today?
- Is there a conversation you need to have—or a door you need to close?
- What action will you take to honor the love you truly deserve?

Final Note:

This reflection is your mirror and your permission slip. You don't have to carry what isn't yours. You don't have to stay seated where you're not being served. The moment you stand up for yourself, you teach others how to treat you, and you remind yourself what you're worthy of.

10

Recognizing Unhealthy Patterns Without Losing Yourself

There comes a point when you stop calling it "bad luck" or "just the way he is" and start calling it what it is—a pattern.

For years, I found myself making excuses for grown people who didn't want to grow. I convinced myself they just needed love, support, or one more chance. But over time, I realized this: you cannot love someone into emotional maturity. You cannot pray, hope, or carry someone into accountability if they're not willing to do the work themselves.

Some men—and some people in general—will take and take until you are completely empty. Not because they're evil, but because they've never learned how not to. And I had to learn the hard way that compassion without boundaries becomes self-abandonment.

Let's get clear: not everyone showing up with chaos is a "loser." But if someone's behaviors are costing you your peace, your energy, and your emotional safety—you don't need a label to know it's not love.

Understanding the Patterns (So You Can Stop Explaining Them Away)

1. No Direction, No Drive, No Desire to Do Better

I've dated the man with dreams that never left his lips. A man who talked about starting businesses, taking trips, making changes—but somehow, nothing ever happened. He didn't lack ideas; he lacked follow-through. That wasn't ambition. That was fear in disguise.

People who stay stuck often aren't lazy—they're unhealed. But that doesn't mean you're supposed to sacrifice your future waiting for them to find theirs.

2. The Perpetual Victim

"It's always someone else's fault."

If you've ever loved someone who plays the victim, you know the emotional exhaustion it brings. Everything becomes about what was done to them, never what they are doing to you.

That mindset isn't just draining—it's contagious. You start walking on eggshells, managing their emotions while suppressing your own. And before you know it, you're apologizing for their behavior.

3. Emotionally Fragile, But Unwilling to Grow

You bring up a concern—they shut down.
You offer feedback—they get defensive.
You want connection—they pull away.
They can't handle discomfort, so they avoid anything that

requires emotional depth. That's not sensitivity—it's avoidance. And avoiding growth is a choice. One you don't have to suffer for.

4. No Accountability, Just Excuses

Some people are escape artists. Every mistake is someone else's fault; every broken promise has a reason. But here's the truth: you can have reasons, or you can have results. Not both.

If they can't own their actions, they can't respect your boundaries.

5. Toxic Relationship Cycles

They say they love you, but their love comes with chaos.
Highs and lows. Passion and pain. Push and pull.
Sometimes, they create drama just to feel connected. But you were never meant to confuse intensity with intimacy. If someone only shows up when there's conflict, that's not love—it's emotional turbulence.

6. Financial Irresponsibility as a Red Flag

It's not about income—it's about integrity.
Does he have a plan? A budget? A sense of responsibility?
If someone is reckless with money, it's often a mirror for how they manage emotions, time, and commitments. If everything is urgent, unpaid, or always someone else's fault—run. Your future is too valuable to hand over to someone who can't manage today.

7. No Empathy, No Respect

You explain your feelings. They laugh.
You express your hurt. They deflect.

You cry. They call you dramatic.

That's not love. That's emotional immaturity. Some people never learned to be empathetic—and sadly, some refuse to. But you are not responsible for teaching someone how to care.

What I Had to Learn (And Maybe You Do Too)

- You are not a rehab center.
- You are not a mother to broken men.
- You are not a life coach for emotionally unavailable people.
- You are not their answer—you are your own.

I had to walk away from people I loved. Not because I stopped loving them—but because I finally started loving me.

A Compassionate Truth

People are not always their behaviors. Sometimes trauma speaks louder than intention. But while understanding someone's pain is powerful, it should never come at the cost of your own healing.

You can hold space for their growth without standing in the fire they keep setting.

You can forgive someone without letting them stay.

You can walk away with love and still leave with your dignity intact.

Journal Reflection: Protecting Your Peace Without Losing Your Compassion

- Have you ever excused unhealthy behavior in someone because you saw "potential"? What did it cost you?

- Are you currently over-functioning in a relationship or friendship? Giving more than you're receiving?
- What patterns have you recognized in others that now feel like red flags? Were there any you ignored?
- Are there any of these behavioral patterns you see in yourself? What might be the root cause?
- When have you acted as a rescuer instead of a partner or friend? Why?
- What boundaries do you need to set right now to protect your emotional and mental health?
- Who in your life has shown true transformation? What helped them change—and what was your role in it?

Affirmation

"I release the need to fix others and reclaim my right to peace, love, and emotional safety. I am allowed to walk away from what hurts, even if I understand it."

11

Crossing Boundaries & Breaking Trust

There's a moment—sharp, quiet, unmistakable—when you realize: something sacred has been broken. It might come like thunder: a betrayal, a secret exposed, a decision made without you. Or it might be soft and subtle: a comment that slices, a silence that speaks volumes, a feeling in your gut that you've just been violated.

This is the moment trust is broken. This is when boundaries—those invisible lines you drew to protect your peace—are crossed like they never existed at all. There is a moment — subtle, yet seismic — when something once sacred becomes shattered.

It doesn't always come with fanfare. Sometimes, it's a whisper. A tone shift. The door was left slightly open. Other times, it's a full-frontal collision: a betrayal, a lie, an act that disrespects our unspoken agreements. This is the realm of broken trust. This is where boundaries — those sacred lines we draw in the sand of our souls — are crossed, smudged, or deliberately erased.

When you're a giver, you want to believe people won't take more than you offer. But takers don't come with warning signs. They come with charm, promises, and sometimes, need so convincing it feels like love. And when they take advantage of your kindness, they chip away at your self-worth. They don't just break rules. They break the parts of you that still believe in loyalty.

But here's the truth: You don't rebuild by going backward. You don't restore trust by reopening the door for someone who kicked it down.

You know the feeling. It hurt. Deep. The sting, the shock that spirals into disorientation. A violation that echoes louder the closer the violator is to your heart. Friends, lovers, family, mentors — when they cross lines without permission, it creates a scar. A narrative rewrite.

"I didn't think they would do this to me."

"I told them what I needed."

"I thought I mattered more."

This chapter is not just about betrayal by others. It's also about the betrayal we sometimes permit — or even participate in — because we're still learning what it means to stand fully in our power.

Let's be honest. How many times have you said "yes" when your entire body screamed "no"? How many times have you allowed someone to chip away at your dignity, inch by inch, wrapped in smiles and promises? How often did you downplay your pain just to keep the peace?

And then, someone crossed the line. Boundaries are not walls. They are bridges — designed to support connection without sacrificing safety. When someone storms across your bridge without invitation, they fracture the structure. And if they do it often enough, the bridge collapses.

Breaking trust isn't just a moment — it's a ripple.

Suddenly, you question everything. You question your judgment. Your memory. Your worth. The world tilts, and the internal narrative becomes infected:

- "Did I cause this?"
- "Maybe I'm too sensitive."
- "This is just how relationships are..."

No. It is not your job to explain away someone else's disrespect.

No. You are not too sensitive — you are aware.

No. This is not love if it demands your silence.

You get to decide where the line is. And you get to hold it with unwavering strength, even when your voice shakes or you have to walk away.

Boundaries are sacred. They are not punishments. They are declarations. They say, "I value myself." They say, "I've done the work." They say, "If you love me, you will respect this line."

When someone repeatedly violates your boundaries, they are showing you who they are. And your job isn't to fix them—it's to listen. Listen to your body. Your spirit. Your exhaustion.

Reclaim your power by honoring the lessons. Rebuild your trust in yourself—not them.

Forgiveness? Maybe. Reconciliation? Optional. But restoration of your peace? Non-negotiable.

Forgiveness may come. Or it may not. That's not the assignment right now.

The assignment is this: Rebuild your boundaries. Reclaim your trust in yourself.

You are not broken because someone failed you.

You are awakening.

Journal Reflections: Reclaiming Your Power

- Recall a time when someone clearly crossed a boundary you set. How did it feel, emotionally and physically?
- What did you tell yourself to justify their behavior at the time? Were you protecting them at your own expense?
- How did that experience impact your sense of self-worth and safety?
- What would you do differently now with the wisdom you've gained?
- What are three boundaries you are committed to upholding in your relationships from now on?
- Write a declaration of self-trust—a statement that honors your growth and your right to protect your peace.

Affirmation

"My boundaries are not up for negotiation. I trust myself to recognize red flags, speak my truth, and walk away when I am not respected. I am not difficult—I am discerning. I am not broken—I am healing. And I deserve peace."

12

A Loveless Relationship

A loveless relationship rarely begins that way.
It often starts with tenderness, shared dreams, and moments that feel like home. But over time, something shifts. Not in a loud, crashing kind of way—but in silence. In glances that no longer linger. In conversations that feel more like chores than connection. In the aching realization that you're lying next to someone, yet feel completely alone.

It's a quiet kind of heartbreak.

You may share a home. A schedule. Even children. You may laugh at the same shows or plan vacations together. But when you lie in bed at night, there's a growing emptiness—a question echoing in your chest: Is this all there is?

Being in a loveless relationship doesn't mean you've failed.

It means something deeply human: you're craving intimacy, connection, and emotional truth. And you owe it to yourself to pay attention.

How Do You Know When Love Has Left the Room?

Start with the questions your spirit already whispers:

- Do I feel emotionally safe and seen with this person?
- When we talk, is it real communication—or just logistics and surface talk?
- Are there unresolved hurts we keep tiptoeing around?
- Has trust been fractured? Is there space for honesty?
- What does physical affection look like now? Is there desire, or just distance?

But also—how do I feel about myself in this relationship?

Do I feel cherished? Heard? Supported? Or do I feel like I've been shrinking just to make it all work?

The Cost of Staying Numb

Being in a loveless relationship takes a toll on your body, your mind, and your soul. You may begin to notice:

- Emotional fatigue or numbness
- Resentment simmering just beneath the surface
- Anxiety, sadness, or that feeling of being "stuck"
- Trouble sleeping, headaches, fatigue, or just a sense of always being "off"
- A fading version of yourself you no longer recognize

What hurts most isn't always the absence of love—it's the memory of it. The hunger for a connection that used to be there. The grief of missing someone who's still in the room.

To Stay or To Leave? The Question That Haunts

There's no easy answer here. But don't skip the hard truths:

- Is there a willingness—on both sides—to repair the relationship?
- Or are you carrying the emotional weight alone?
- Are you staying because you love them—or because you're afraid of being alone?
- If you have children, are they witnessing a healthy model of love—or a version that teaches them to settle?

Hope is beautiful. But hope without action is a trap.

You can hope for healing and protect your peace at the same time.

If You Choose to Leave—You Are Not Failing

Leaving isn't giving up. It's waking up.

It's choosing honesty over illusion. Peace over pretense.

If your soul knows it's time:

- Gather your support circle. Confide in someone who truly sees you.
- Create a safety and transition plan. One step at a time.
- Find shelter—in a friend's home, with family, or through organizations that offer safety.

You don't have to rush. But you do have to listen to yourself.

Practical Steps to Reclaim Your Life

- Set a timeline. Honor your pace—there is no right or wrong.
- Take what matters: documents, keepsakes, items tied to your identity and safety.

- Communicate boundaries clearly. Emotional, physical, digital.
- Know your legal rights. Seek counsel if finances, assets, or children are involved.
- Make a budget. Understand your new financial landscape and plan from a place of strength.

You may feel unsure at first—but clarity will come. And so will your confidence.

Healing Begins With You

The grief will come in waves. So will the relief.

Some days you'll miss the routine, even the familiarity of dysfunction. That's normal. But in time, you'll begin to feel something deeper—yourself returning to you.

- Therapy can help you process what happened and what it meant.
- Support groups remind you that you're not alone.
- Spiritual practices, journaling, movement, or even sitting in silence can reconnect you to your core.

You're not starting over. You're starting again—this time, with wisdom.

Reclaiming Joy After Loss

Healing isn't just about pain—it's about rediscovery.

- What makes you laugh uncontrollably?
- What did you love before you lost yourself in the relationship?
- What version of you have you missed most?

Try something new. Say "yes" to small joys. Take back your mornings, your playlists, your peace. Each act of self-care is an act of resistance. A rebellion against numbness. A homecoming to you.

Moving Forward with Grace

Forgiveness doesn't mean returning. Nor does it mean "re-engagement."

"It means freeing yourself from the weight of the past." ("Forgiving doesn't mean forgetting —it means freeing ... - Facebook")

Forgive yourself for not leaving sooner. For trying too hard. For not knowing what you know now.

Set boundaries so clear, they can be seen in the dark.

What you left behind doesn't define you.

What you're building now—that's the legacy.

Journal Reflection: What Does Love Look Like—To You?

Use these questions as a mirror to your heart. Be honest. Be gentle. Be brave.

- How do I truly feel in this relationship?
- When was the last time I felt emotionally nourished?
- What efforts have I made—and what efforts have been returned?
- What parts of myself have I muted or lost to keep this relationship afloat?
- What am I afraid will happen if I leave?
- What am I sacrificing by staying?
- What does my version of love, safety, and connection look like?

- If a friend shared this story with me, what would I tell them?
- What would it feel like to live in a relationship that feeds me emotionally, spiritually, and physically?
- What is one loving action I can take today—to honor myself?

Affirmation

"I am worthy of love that feels like truth.

I no longer chase connection where it cannot grow.

I release the need to prove, to fix, or to settle.

I return to myself—fully, freely, unapologetically.

Peace is my new companion. And joy is finding me again."

13

When It's Not Progressing—It's Time to Pivot (and Peace Out)

There comes a time when you realize you've been giving too much for far too little. I've lived that moment. For too long, I played roles I was never meant to audition for: cook, caretaker, co-signer, counselor, chauffeur, lover, lifeline... all without the title, the commitment, or the reciprocation.

And why? Because I wanted a connection. I wanted to believe. I wanted to build something real, not realizing I was laying bricks while he brought only empty hands and big expectations.

In every relationship, you will find that moment when you must pause and ask yourself:

Am I being loved the way I deserve, or am I simply being tolerated?

One of the most common mistakes women make is giving "wife energy" to someone offering nothing more than "boyfriend crumbs." You give. You support. You stay. Meanwhile, he coasts — doing the bare minimum if that. And in that quiet erosion of your needs, your worth begins to feel negotiable.

But hear this: Your worth is not up for debate.

Let's keep it real—love is supposed to grow you, not grind you down. Relationships should elevate, not exhaust. But if you've been pouring, fixing, explaining, and compromising until you're emotionally wrung out while the other person's just...coasting? Yeah. We've got a problem.

There comes a point when the emotional math just doesn't add up anymore.

And when that happens, you owe it to yourself to stop asking "what more can I do?" and start asking "why am I still here?"

This isn't about bitterness. It's about boundaries.

And it's about reclaiming your power with a little sass and a whole lot of clarity.

Communication or Just Lip Service?

If the conversation always feels like you're talking to a wall— or worse, into a void of defensiveness, dismissiveness, or dead air—it's not communication. It's emotional bread crumbing.

Let's be honest:

- Are you being heard, or are you being handled?
- Do they listen—or just wait for their turn to defend?

If all you're getting are dry responses and recycled arguments, guess what? You're not evolving together. You're rerunning a rerun. Time to change the channel.

Emotional Intimacy or Cold Roommate Vibes?

Intimacy isn't just physical—it's emotional safety. It's laughing in your bonnet. It's crying without shame. It's being raw, real, and still accepted.

If you're starting to feel like live-in strangers or emotionally disconnected business partners... that's not love. That's logistics.

If every attempt to connect is met with apathy, neglect, or deflection—you're not in a relationship, you're in a holding pattern.

Do Your Goals Still Align—or Are You Just Aligned on the Lease?

You don't need to want all the same things, but your vision can't clash on every major decision. If you want growth and they want comfort, if you want purpose and they want autopilot, you're forcing a future that's already waving red flags.

Ask yourself:

- Are we still moving in the same direction?
- Or am I the only one holding the map?

Effort Check: Are You Building Solo?

A healthy relationship isn't 50/50—it's 100/100. Two people showing up for real.

If you're always the initiator, always the emotional mule, always the one sacrificing, while they show up when it's convenient—stop calling that love. That's a hustle, and you're the product.

You weren't made to carry a connection all by yourself. If they can't meet you halfway, it's okay to walk the full way out.

Not Every Love Is Meant to Last Forever

Some relationships are seasonal. They come to teach, to stretch, to awaken. But when the lesson is learned, keeping the relationship becomes a choice between growth or guilt.

If the future feels foggy and forced, it's not fear—it's your intuition whispering, "This ain't it."

Time to Reevaluate—With No Apologies

Let go of blame. This is about truth, not shame.

Speak up. Express what's real. Pay attention to what comes back. Are they willing to do the work, or are they just good at saying what you want to hear?

Sometimes evaluation leads to reconnection. Other times, it leads to your exit.

Either way, you win—because clarity is freedom.

Get Support, Not Noise

Everyone has an opinion. Choose who gets access.

Talk to people who actually know you, who love your wholeness, not just your ability to keep the peace. That friend who says, "You don't deserve this"? Listen to her.

Support is wisdom. Use it.

If You're Leaving—Do It With Power

If it's time to go, don't tiptoe. Pivot with purpose.

- Get your exit strategy.
- Make your peace.
- Set your boundaries.
- And don't explain your healing to people committed to misunderstanding your pain.

Walking away isn't weakness. It's the loudest declaration of self-love you'll ever make.

Journal Reflections: Real Talk Edition
Grab a pen. Get honest. No sugarcoating.

- What red flags have I been downplaying?
- What would I tell my best friend if they were in this same relationship?
- When I picture staying, do I feel peace or pressure?
- What part of me have I quieted just to "keep the peace"?
- What am I afraid of—and what would happen if I faced that fear head-on?
- Am I settling out of love… or out of habit?
- What's the cost of staying another year?
- What would choosing me look and feel like, right now?

Affirmation: Enough Is Enough
"I am not here to carry dead weight.
I am not here to beg for effort, attention, or honesty.
I am the table, the feast, and the whole damn room.
If you can't grow with me, don't stand in my way.
I am choosing me—fully, freely, and without apology.
Good love will find me. Until then, kick rocks."

14

The Moment of Liberation —When a Woman Gets Up From the Table

There is a sacred moment—quiet, but unshakable—when a woman decides to stop waiting for permission to be free.
Not free in the eyes of others.
Free in her spirit.
Free from the need to shrink, twist, or bargain for love.

This chapter is about that moment. The knowing. The choosing. The rising.

It's the moment when you finally say: "Enough is enough. I refuse to dim my light. I refuse to beg for crumbs when I was born to feast. This table—this situation, this person, this version of me—no longer serves the woman I am becoming. And I choose me."

The Spark: A Soul-Wide Awakening
Liberation doesn't always come dressed in fireworks. Some-

times, it's a whisper from within: "You were never meant to live like this."

Maybe it started with the way your laughter faded. Maybe it was the ache in your chest that wouldn't go away. Or maybe it was the realization that your joy was always on hold—contingent on someone else's approval. No more.

This chapter is not about betrayal. It's about breakthrough.

It's not about blame. It's about becoming.

It's about that breath you take when you finally walk out of the shadows and into the sunlight of your own truth. That breath is yours now.

Reclaiming the Table—or Walking Away from It

Ask yourself this:

"Is this still a table of nourishment—or is it now a table of depletion?"

You've tried. You've compromised. You've prayed, cried, endured, and sacrificed. But if what's being served is pain, silence, and emotional scraps—then it's time to push back your chair, stand tall, and rise.

Because a liberated woman doesn't eat where she's not respected. She creates a new table. One with love, truth, abundance, and joy as the centerpiece.

Boundaries: Your Sacred YES and NO

You don't owe anyone an explanation for choosing peace.

You don't need permission to declare your worth.

Boundaries are not barriers—they're bridges. They reconnect you to the parts of yourself you once silenced to keep the peace. Speak them with power. Honor them like vows. And know this: Protecting your peace is not selfish. It is sacred.

The Joy of Choosing You

Let's celebrate this: you got up!

You got up from the table that demanded your silence, your sacrifice, your soul.

You got up with trembling legs, maybe—but with a spirit that said: "I was not created to suffer. I was created to soar."

And now? There is a glow about you. A fire. A freedom.

Not just because you left—but because you remembered who you are. And you made peace with the truth that being fully you is not too much. It's your superpower.

This Is What Liberation Feels Like

- It feels like laughter in your belly again.
- It feels like sleeping peacefully through the night.
- It feels like turning your phone off without fear.
- It feels like wearing red lipstick for you.
- It feels like joy, unapologetically, abundantly, endlessly.

Liberation is not loud—it's light. It is peace that no one can snatch from your hands ever again.

You Are Not the Wound. You Are the Warrior.

You don't need closure when you are the closing chapter.

You don't need them to say sorry when your spirit already whispered: "Let's go."

You don't need to explain your decision to rise.

Because freedom doesn't require an audience—it just requires a decision.

And sis, you made it.

Journal Reflections

- What part of me feels most alive now that I've chosen myself?
- What version of me is finally free to emerge?
- How can I celebrate my decision to rise instead of mourning what I've walked away from?
- What relationships now deserve a front-row seat in my life—and which need to remain in the past?
- What does it feel like to live as the woman I was always meant to be?

Affirmation

"I am not the pain—I am the possibility.

I am not the past—I am the promise.

I did not break—I broke free.

And with every step forward, I claim my joy, my peace, and my power.

This is my moment. I have risen. And I'm never going back."

15

When Love Isn't Being Served – Take Your Seat Somewhere Else

I can't tell you when it's time to go... or when it's time to stay. That's not my decision to make.

This is *your* story. *Your* truth. Or... maybe even the lies you've whispered to yourself to make it through another day.

But I will tell you this: if you're reading this, then you're already starting to feel that shift—the soft rumble in your spirit that says, *"Something here no longer serves me."*

And that whisper is never wrong.

"When love is no longer being served, it's time to get up from the table."

A certain ache comes with realizing you've stayed too long.

But there's also sweet, liberating peace in knowing you've finally chosen *yourself*.

Will it hurt? Probably.

Will it feel like salt in the wound? Definitely.

But here's the grace in it: **the wound will heal.**

You won't always feel the sting. One day, you'll touch that scar and smile—not because you loved the pain, but because you *survived* it.

You meet people who are attracted to your "shine." But the minute they get you, they knowingly or unknowingly work to diminish that shine. It's kinda ironic. The very thing that drew them to you becomes the very thing they despise or can't handle.

Here's what I do know for certain:

- Never put all your eggs in one basket. That applies to love, finances, dreams, and plans.
- Always—always—save for your rainy day. Because when the storm hits, you'll need your own umbrella, not someone else's permission to stand under theirs.
- Inspect what you expect.
- Don't just listen to what people say—watch what they do. Because sometimes, it's not about speaking up… It's about sitting back and observing.
- "When someone shows you who they are, believe them the first time." ("20 Maya Angelou Quotes to Uplift and Inspire You - Reader's Digest") – Maya Angelou.
- Never beg and never chase the love that has to be hunted down and dragged back.
- I didn't say to be so guarded or puffed-up that you block everyone out, but you must know your worth. Not in theory. In practice.
- Love is not crumbs.
- Love is not confusion.
- Love is not pain dressed up in pretty promises.

- You are not too much, too broken, too loud, too anything. You are exactly right for the one who truly sees you.
- Sometimes you'll have to make uncomfortable decisions, but they are necessary. And when that time comes, make sure your finances are tight. Make sure your spirit is grounded.
- Keep your circle close. Everyone smiling at you isn't celebrating with you.
- "Not everyone at your table is your friend. Some just came for the food."
- Yes, there's a lot to consider.
- But in the end, it comes down to one thing: your happiness.
- What are you willing to accept?
- What are you willing to fight for?
- And most importantly… what are you no longer willing to tolerate?
- "You don't lose them when you leave. You find you."

So, don't be afraid to stand up if you're sitting at a table where love is not being served. Walk away with grace. With dignity. With clarity.

Because sometimes the most radical act of love is choosing yourself.

And baby, that's not selfish. That's sacred. That's authentic! That's Self-Love!

16

Author's Favorite Quotes

- Don't dare shrink yourself for someone else's comfort.
- Do not become small for people who refuse to grow.
- Never dim your shine, because someone else sees you as competition.
- "Create Your Future"
- Never believe in a one-sided story. It has some pages missing.
- Don't worry about what people say behind your back.
- You don't have to set yourself on fire to keep others warm.
- Don't let loneliness & desperation make you ignore the red flags in relationships.
- No means NO!

Epilogue

A Sacred Beginning

There is something holy about the moment you finally say, "No more."

Not out of anger, but out of clarity. Not from bitterness, but from wisdom. That moment—when you rise from the table—is not the end of your story. It's the divine beginning of a new one.

You may not have all the answers. You may still feel the sting of loss, the ache of letting go, the tremble of uncertainty. But know this: you are not broken—you are breaking through.

Walking away isn't weakness. It's spiritual strength. It's choosing peace over pretending, truth over tolerance, and soul over survival. It's remembering that your worth is not up for negotiation. You were not created to shrink, settle, or silence your spirit just to keep someone else comfortable.

My prayer is that you now recognize the power within you. That you trust your intuition more. That you love yourself more deeply. That you know that healing isn't about going back to who you were but awakening to who you are becoming.

This book may end here, but your journey continues—with your head held high and your heart wide open.

So, rise, beloved. Walk forward. The table you deserve is waiting.

WHEN TO GET UP FROM THE TABLE-WHEN LOVE IS NOT BEING SERVED

— Gloria Bailey-Ray

Afterword

From My Heart to Yours

When I began writing this book, I had no idea how deeply I would be called to revisit my own moments of pain, revelation, and liberation. Each chapter pulled something sacred from within me—pieces of my truth I had once hidden, softened, or silenced.

This wasn't just a writing journey. It was a soul journey.
   And if you're reading these final words, I want to thank you for walking it with me.

When To Get Up From The Table was written for the woman who's questioning her worth, the man who's staying out of fear, the soul that knows it's time to go—but needs a reminder that they are not alone. This book is a mirror, a map, and a call to remember: you were never meant to settle in spaces that dishonor your spirit.

To those who have supported me—family, friends, clients, sisters in struggle and in strength—thank you. Your stories, your resilience, and your courage inspired these pages more than you'll ever know.

I hope this book doesn't just sit on a shelf.

I hope it travels.

I hope it becomes underlined, dog-eared, wept over, and passed on.

I hope it awakens the one thing we all need more of: self-love that tells the truth.

This is not goodbye. It's an invitation.

To rise. To rebuild. To walk into the next chapter—unapologetically authentic.

With love and truth,
   Gloria Bailey-Ray

About the Author

Meet Gloria Bailey-Ray — The Authentic Coach

Gloria Bailey-Ray is a dynamic author, Certified Professional Coach, acclaimed keynote speaker, and the powerhouse behind It's Essential, LLC. With over 30 years of experience across corporate, coaching, and media landscapes, Gloria has become a respected voice for transformation, resilience, and leadership.

She is best known as "The Authentic Coach"—a fierce advocate for helping others reclaim their voice, step into confidence, and rise unapologetically into their purpose. Her straight talk, humor, and magnetic presence captivate audiences of all ages and backgrounds—from C-suite executives to grassroots changemakers.

Gloria is also the creator, producer, and longtime host of The Gloria Bailey-Ray Show, a platform that has empowered thousands through bold conversations on healing, career growth, relationships, and personal power.

Author of the Transformational Book

When To Get Up From The Table: When Love Is Not Being Served

Gloria's most personal and powerful book yet, When To Get Up From The Table, is a raw and soul-stirring invitation to rise after betrayal, reclaim self-worth, and transform pain into purpose. It's more than a book—it's a movement of liberation and self-love.

She is also the author of two other books focused on empowerment and transformational growth.

You can connect with me on:

- https://www.gloriabaileyray.com
- https://www.linkedin.com/in/gloriabaileyray
- https://www.facebook.com/gbaileyray
- http://www.youtube.com/c/GloriaBaileyRay

Subscribe to my newsletter:

- http://www.constantcontact.com/index.jsp?cc=forms_inline

www.ingramcontent.com/pod-product-compliance
Lightning Source LLC
Chambersburg PA
CBHW071251070526
44583CB00017B/2420